MW01519112

Too Cute!

Baby Kangaroos

by Betsy Rathburn

BLASTOFF!
Beginners

BELLWETHER MEDIA
MINNEAPOLIS, MN

Blastoff! Beginners are developed by literacy experts and educators to meet the needs of early readers. These engaging informational texts support young children as they begin reading about their world. Through simple language and high frequency words paired with crisp, colorful photos, Blastoff! Beginners launch young readers into the universe of independent reading.

Blastoff! Universe

Reading Level

Grade K

Grades 1-3

Grade 4

Sight Words in This Book 🔍

a	eat	jump	them
and	get	look	they
are	has	other	this
at	in	play	to
big	is	soon	up
called	it	the	with

This edition first published in 2024 by Bellwether Media, Inc.

No part of this publication may be reproduced in whole or in part without written permission of the publisher. For information regarding permission, write to Bellwether Media, Inc., Attention: Permissions Department, 6012 Blue Circle Drive, Minnetonka, MN 55343.

Library of Congress Cataloging-in-Publication Data

Names: Rathburn, Betsy, author.
Title: Baby kangaroos / by Betsy Rathburn.
Description: Minneapolis, MN : Bellwether Media, Inc., 2024. | Series: Blastoff! Beginners. Too cute! | Includes bibliographical references and index. | Audience: Ages PreK-2 | Audience: Grades K-1
Identifiers: LCCN 2023000126 (print) | LCCN 2023000127 (ebook) | ISBN 9798886874051 (library binding) | ISBN 9798886875935 (ebook)
Subjects: LCSH: Kangaroos--Infancy--Juvenile literature.
Classification: LCC QL737.M35 R36 2024 (print) | LCC QL737.M35 (ebook) |
DDC 599.2/221392--dc23/eng/20230105
LC record available at https://lccn.loc.gov/2023000126
LC ebook record available at https://lccn.loc.gov/2023000127

Text copyright © 2024 by Bellwether Media, Inc. BLASTOFF! BEGINNERS and associated logos are trademarks and/or registered trademarks of Bellwether Media, Inc.

Editor: Rachael Barnes   Designer: Laura Sowers

Printed in the United States of America, North Mankato, MN.

Table of Contents

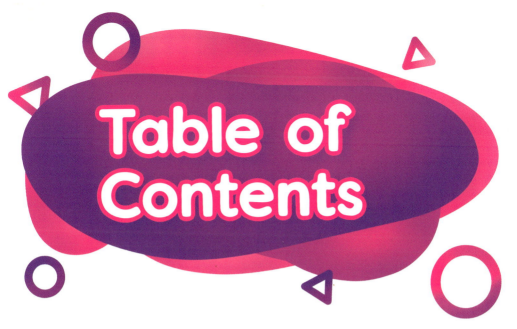

A Baby Kangaroo!

Look at the
baby kangaroo.
Hello, joey!

Life with Mom

Newborn joeys are tiny. They stay in mom's **pouch**.

newborn

pouch

They get bigger.
They grow hair.
They peek
outside.

They start
to eat grass.
Mom carries them.

Soon they leave mom's pouch. They walk and hop!

hopping

They live
in groups
called **mobs**.
They stay safe.

mob

They play with
other joeys.
They learn
to **box**!

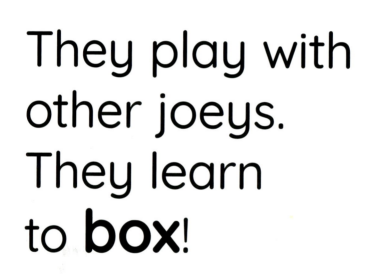

boxing

All Grown Up!

Joeys grow.
They get big feet
and strong tails.

This joey is
grown up.
It has
a big jump!

jumping

Baby Kangaroo Facts

Kangaroo Life Stages

newborn   joey   adult

A Day in the Life

eat grass   hop   box

Glossary

box

to fight another kangaroo

mobs

groups of kangaroos

newborn

just born

pouch

a pocket on the belly of a mother kangaroo

To Learn More

ON THE WEB

FACTSURFER

Factsurfer.com gives you a safe, fun way to find more information.

1. Go to www.factsurfer.com.

2. Enter "baby kangaroos" into the search box and click 🔍.

3. Select your book cover to see a list of related content.

Index